W9-ABH-019

WITHDRAWN
L. R. COLLEGE LIBRARY

833.912
M31s

82105

DATE DUE			
Apr28 '75			

A LIST OF

The Principal Works of Thomas Mann

will be found

at the end of this volume

A Sketch of My Life

A Sketch of My Life

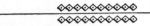

THOMAS MANN

<small>TRANSLATED FROM THE GERMAN BY</small>

H. T. Lowe-Porter

1 9  7 0

ALFRED A. KNOPF · NEW YORK

CARL A. RUDISILL LIBRARY
LENOIR RHYNE COLLEGE

833.912
M3 1s
82105
Feb. 1973

L. C. Catalog card number: 60–11424

This is a BORZOI BOOK, *published by* ALFRED A. KNOPF, INC.

All rights reserved under International and Pan-American Copyright Conventions. Published in the United States by Alfred A. Knopf, Inc., New York, and in Canada by Random House of Canada Limited, Toronto. Manufactured in the United States of America and distributed by Random House, Inc., New York.

PUBLISHED AUGUST 15, 1960

SECOND PRINTING, DECEMBER, 1970

Originally published in German as "Lebensabriss" in *Die Neue Rundschau*, S. Fischer, Berlin, July 7, 1930. Subsequently published in English in a limited edition by Harrison of Paris in October 1930.

A Sketch of My Life

◆◇◆◇◆◇◆◇◆◇◆

T

◇◇◇◇◇◇◇◇◇◇◇◇◇◇◇◇◇◇◇◇◇

M

I WAS BORN in Lübeck in the year 1875, the second son of Johann Heinrich Mann, merchant and Senator of the Free City, and of his wife, Julia Da Silva-Bruhns. My father, grandfather, and great-grandfather were citizens of Lübeck; but my mother first saw the light in Rio de Janeiro, the daughter of a German planter and a Portuguese-Creole Brazilian, and was brought to Germany when she was seven years old. She was distinctly Latin in type, in her youth a much-admired beauty, and extraordinarily musical. When I ask myself the hereditary origin of my characteristics I am fain to recall Goethe's famous little

4

verse and say that I too have from my father *"des Lebens ernstes Führen,"* but from my mother the *"Frohnatur"*—the sensuous, artistic side, and, in the widest sense, the *"Lust zu fabulieren."*

My childhood was sheltered and happy. We five children, three boys and two girls, grew up in a spacious and dignified house built by my father; but we had a second home in the old family dwelling beside Saint Mary's, where my paternal grandmother lived alone, and which today is shown to the curious as "the Buddenbrook house." The brightest hours of my youth were those summer holidays at Travemünde on the Baltic bay: with the mornings spent bathing at the beach, and the afternoons, almost as passionately loved, by the steps of the bandstand opposite the gardens of the hotel. That idyllic life—well-tended, carefree, with many-coursed table-d'hôte meals—appealed to me inexpressibly. It encouraged my native tendency to idleness and dreams—corrected much later and with difficulty; and when the four weeks, which had seemed a little eternity when they began, were over and we returned to daily life, my breast was torn with tender, self-pitying pangs.

School I loathed, and to the end failed to satisfy its demands. I despised it as a milieu, I was critical of the manners of its masters, and I early espoused a sort of literary opposition to its spirit, its discipline, and its methods of training. My indolence, necessary perhaps to my particular growth; my need of much free time for leisure and quiet reading; an actual heaviness of spirit—even today I suffer from it—made me hate being urged to study, and react with feelings of contempt and scorn.

The humanities might have proved better suited to my needs; but I was intended for a merchant—the heir to the old family business—and so attended the Realgymnasium at the Katherineum, where I got no further than qualifying for the one-year military-service certificate—that is to say, as far as the upper second. During almost the whole of this stagnating, unsatisfying time I had for a friend the son of a Lübeck bookseller who had failed in business and then died. Our friendship subsisted on a fantastic and scurrilous mockery of "the whole thing" but in particular the "institution" and its heads.

. . .

Among these it injured me much that I "wrote." I had not been discreet enough, probably out of vanity. I had boastfully shown to one of my fellow pupils a romance whose theme was the heroic death of Arria: *"Paete, non dolet,"* and he, half in admiration and half in malice, turned it over to a master. Thus, while I was still in the lower third, my troublesome unconformity was made plain to the authorities.

I had begun with childish plays, which I and my younger brothers and sisters performed before our parents and aunts. Then there were poems, inscribed to a dear friend, the one who as Hans Hansen, in *Tonio Kröger*, has a sort of symbolic existence, though in real life he took to drink and made a melancholy end in Africa. What became of the flaxen-haired dancing partner who later was the object of love lyrics, I cannot say.

Only much later did I try to write tales, and then it was after a phase of critical essays: when I was in the second form I and some radical-minded first-formers got out a periodical called *Der Frühlingssturm (Spring Storm)*— not a very proper school paper, I fear—wherein I chiefly shone as a writer of philosophic and revolutionary articles.

Five years ago I visited Lübeck, on the Free City's seven hundredth anniversary, and renewed acquaintance with the master of the lower second who also had taught Latin and German. I told the snowy-haired Emeritus that I knew he had always found me a thorough good-for-nothing, but that I had quietly taken in a good deal in his classes nonetheless. And in evidence I cited the set phrase in which he always extolled to us Schiller's ballads: "This is not just *any* reading you are having; it is the very best reading you could have!" "Did I say that?" he cried, greatly delighted.

My father died a relatively young man, of blood-poisoning, when I was fifteen. Thanks to his intelligence and his superior bearing, he had always been a highly respected, popular, and influential citizen. But his business for some time had not gone very well, and the hundred-year-old grain firm went into liquidation not long after a funeral which in size and pomp surpassed anything that had been seen in Lübeck for many years. We sold the town house, as my grandmother's had been sold before it, and moved from that spacious home, where in the parquetry ballroom the officers of the garrison had courted the daughters of the patriciate, into a comparatively modest villa with a garden, outside the city gate. My mother, however, soon left the town for good and all. She loved the south, the mountains, Munich, whither she once had travelled with my father; and to Munich she moved with my younger brothers and sisters, leaving me to board with a professor's family. There I lived, with some scions of Mecklenburg and Holstein landed nobility and gentry, until my school life gradually dwindled to an end.

Of this period I have the most jovial memories. The "institution" had given up all hope for me. It left me to my fate, and that was dark to me; but, feeling myself quite hearty and clever, I was not cast down. I sat away the hours. Outside school I lived very much as I liked, and stood well with my fellow boarders, in whose premature drinking bouts I gaily condescended to take part now and then. In the fulness of time I got my certificate and took my leave, following my family to Munich, where, with the word "temporary" in my heart, I entered an insurance office managed by a friend of my father, who had earlier carried on the same kind of business in Lübeck.

A singular interlude. I sat at my sloping desk surrounded by snuff-taking clerks and copied out accounts; but secretly I also wrote my first tale, a love story called *Gefallen*. It earned me my first literary success. For not only was it published in *Die Gesellschaft*, M. G. Conrad's radical-naturalistic polemical monthly, which—while I was still at school—had published a poem of mine that pleased the young; but the story also brought me a warmhearted and encouraging letter from Richard Dehmel and later even a visit from that much-admired poet. His benevolent enthusiasm had found hints of talent in my painfully immature but perhaps not quite unmelodious little offering; and from that time until his death he followed my progress with sympathy, friendship, and flattering prophecies.

My business activities, which I had always looked upon

as a stopgap, came to an end after a year. With the help of my mother's lawyer, who had confidence in me, I won my freedom. Encouraged by him, I came out with my desire to be a "journalist." I registered at the University and attended lectures which seemed likely to forward me in the rather indefinite calling I proposed: courses in history, political economy, literature, and art. From time to time I attended these with fair regularity and not quite without profit. I was particularly enthusiastic over a course on the court epic by Wilhelm Herz, the poet and translator from Middle High German.

Without being formally a student at the University, I lived like one. In the lecture room I got acquainted with members of the University Dramatic Club, and joined a coffee-house group interested in poetry and the drama, among whom I enjoyed a little esteem as the author of *Gefallen*. The student I saw most of was a young North German law student named Koch, a clever chap who became a lawyer and later the burgomaster of Cassel. Under the name Koch-Weser he has had an important political career: after the Revolution he became Home Secretary, and is today the leader of the Democratic Party of Germany.

Even established authors and writers sometimes visited our youthful group: Otto Erich Hartleben, Istrati Panizza, J. Schaumberger, L. Scharf, old Heinrich von Reder. The most important event during my time was the first German performance of Ibsen's *The Wild Duck;* Ernst von Wolzogen produced it for the club, and it had a literary success despite the protests of a conservative public. Wolzogen played old Ekdal, Hans Olden the writer was Hjalmar, and I, in Wolzogen's fur coat and spectacles, took the part of Werle the wholesale merchant. At later meetings Wolzogen used to remark facetiously that he had discovered me.

My brother Heinrich, four years older than I, later to be the author of such important and significant novels, was living in Rome and, like me, "biding his time." He suggested my joining him, and I did: we lived as few Germans do, through a long, scorching Italian summer, in a little town in the Sabine Hills—Palestrina, birthplace of the composer.

The winter, with its alternation of cutting tramontana and sultry sirocco days, we spent in the Eternal City, renting rooms from an old woman who had a flat with stone floors and wicker chairs on the Via Torre Argentina. We had our meals at a little restaurant named Genzano—I have looked for it since but could not find it—where we got good wine and capital "*crocchette di pollo.*" Evenings we went to a café, played dominoes, and drank punch. We made no friends. If we heard German spoken, we fled.

We regarded Rome as the refuge of our irregularity, and I, at least, lived there not on account of the south, which at bottom I did not love, but quite simply because there was no room yet for me at home. I accepted respectfully the historical and aesthetic impressions the city had to offer, but scarcely with the feeling that they concerned me or had immediate significance for me. The antique statues in the Vatican meant more to me than the painting of the Renaissance. *The Last Judgement* thrilled me: it was the apotheosis of my entirely pessimistic, moralizing, anti-hedonistic frame of mind. I enjoyed going to

Saint Peter's and hearing Cardinal Rampolla, the Papal
Secretary of State, in all the pride of his humility read
mass. He was an uncommonly decorative personage, and
on aesthetic grounds I later felt sorry that diplomatic con-
siderations prevented his elevation to the Chair of Saint
Peter.

Our mother enjoyed the income of a moderate middle-
class fortune, whose heirs we children were, according to
my father's will. She gave us brothers a hundred and sixty
or eighty marks a month each, a remittance which improved in the Italian exchange and to us meant a great
deal: economic freedom, the power to bide our time. If we
did not want too much, we could do what we wanted—
and we did. My brother, who originally meant to be an
artist, sketched a great deal, while I, in the reek of endless
three-centesimi cigarettes, devoured Scandinavian and
Russian literature and wrote. The successes that gradually
came my way rejoiced me but did not surprise. My attitude toward life was compact of indolence, bad civic conscience, and the sure and certain feeling of latent powers.
In those days I had a letter from Ludwig Jakobowsky, who
was editing *Die Gesellschaft* in Leipzig. I had sent him a

story, and his reply began: "What a gifted creature you are!" I laughed at his astonishment, which, curiously enough, I found naïve.

More important still, a story I had finished in Munich, *Little Herr Friedemann*, had pleased them at Fischer's, in Berlin. Oskar Bie, editor of the *Neue Deutsche Rundschau*, wrote about it with interest and asked me to send them what else I had. While I was still in Rome my first book came out, a little volume of short stories that took its title from that earliest one. I could "see myself" in the Roman bookshops.

While living in Palestrina, I had begun to write *Buddenbrooks*—after zealous preparations. I had no great faith in the practical outcome of the enterprise; yet with the patience which my native slowness laid upon me, a phlegm perhaps better described as restrained nervousness, I continued it in Via Torre Argentina, and carried back to Munich a fearsomely swollen bundle of manuscript.

I had been gone nearly a year. At first I lived with my mother, but later in little bachelor quarters which I furnished partly myself and partly with family relics. With my manuscript solemnly laid forth on the extension table which I had draped with green baize, I spent whole days squatting before the wicker chairs I had bought "in the white" and painting them with red enamel. There is a description of such a Bohemian ménage in *The Wardrobe*, a story—written in the Marktstrasse in Schwabing— which first saw the light in the *Neue Deutsche Rundschau*.

Korfiz Holm was at that time a member of the publishing house of Langen, whose head, like Wedekind, was living abroad under a charge of *lèse-majesté*. Holm was Baltic by birth and a friend from Lübeck days, where he had been graduated from the first form. He met me on the street one day and offered me a position on *Simplicissimus*, at a hundred marks a month. For about a year— until Langen, still in Paris, abolished the job I held—I worked as reader and press reader in the fine offices on Schackstrasse. My particular task was to make the first selection from the incoming short-story manuscripts and to submit my suggestions to my superior, Dr. Geheeb, brother of the Landschule educationist. This occupation had some sense. I liked the magazine, had always preferred it to Georg Hirt's *Jugend*, whose sprightliness I found philistine; and had accordingly been made happy by the appearance in two early numbers of a tale of mine, *The Will to Happiness*. I had received the fee, in gold, from young Jakob Wassermann. While my brother and I were in Palestrina we once, in a burst of energy, made a picture book which was a kind of "classicizing" of *Simplicissimus* —its flair for literary caricature, its vein of pessimistic and fantastic humour. Most inappropriately, we sent it to our younger sister for a confirmation present. A few funny sketches from this production, by my own unskilful hand, were published on the occasion of my fiftieth birthday.

Thus, my relations with *Simplicissimus* were not without some fitness. I made myself useful in the editorial offices, while remaining a contributor; several of my short stories, *The Way to the Churchyard* and some others that have not been included in my Collected Works, were printed there, and even a Christmas poem. *The Way to the Churchyard* was particularly liked by Ludwig Thoma, by then already closely connected with *Simplicissimus* and the publishing house. Langen and his subordinates liked even better the highly subjective Schiller study, *A Weary Hour*, which I wrote for *Simplicissimus* on the hundredth anniversary of the poet's death. It astonished and moved me to have Thoma, the South Bavarian folk writer, greet with such earnest and cordial appreciation this little work by an author so much younger and so differently constituted. On my side, I have always heartily loved and admired his *Lausbubengeschichten* and *Filserbriefe*. Now and again I spent an evening in the Odeon Bar with him and other *Simplicissimus* people: Geheeb, Th. Th. Heine, Thöny, Reznicek, among others. Thoma slept most of the time, his cold pipe in his mouth.

I said above that my relation with this flippant and truly artistic sphere—the best "München" there has ever been—was a fitting one. But not all of my nature was involved in it. They had given me the luxury of an office of my own, with a desk for my editorial activities; but alongside these ran the claims of my personal concern, the work on *Buddenbrooks*—to which I entirely devoted myself once more, after my connection with the house of Langen was severed.

I sometimes read aloud out of it to my mother, brothers
and sisters, and friends. It was a family entertainment, like
another. They laughed, and I think I am right in saying
that they thought I was merely amusing myself and them
with this obstinate and ambitious enterprise. At best it was
a protracted finger-exercise, with no ulterior advantages.
I would be at a loss to say whether I thought any differently.

At this time I was close friends with two young people
from my sister's youthful circle, the sons of a Dresden
painter, Professor E—— of the Academy. The younger,
Paul, was also a painter; he was then at the Academy, a
pupil of the famous animal painter Zügel; but he was a
capital violinist as well. My liking for him had originally
something of my former feelings for my blond school-
mate; but, thanks to our having much more in common
mentally and spiritually, the relationship was happier.
Karl, the elder, is today a professional musician and composer and a professor at the Academy at Cologne. While
Paul painted my portrait, Karl in his admirably sustained
and harmonious style would play to us both out of *Tristan*.
Sometimes, as I fiddled a little too, we would play his trios.

We bicycled together, went to the Schwabing "Peasant Balls," or had jolly suppers at my place or theirs. Thanks to them, I learned the pleasures of friendship, as without them I scarcely should have done: gently and tactfully they overcame my heaviness, shyness, and irritability, by accepting them frankly as accompanying phenomena of gifts which they held in respect. Those were precious days.

I was such an impassioned bicycle rider at that time that I scarcely went a step on foot, but even in a pouring rain took my way, in cloak and galoshes, upon my machine. I carried it on my shoulder up the three flights of stairs to my flat, where it lived in the kitchen. Mornings, after my work, I used to stand it on its saddle and clean it. Another task, before I shaved and went to town, was cleaning my oil stove. A charwoman "did" my rooms while I ate my one-mark-twenty meal. Summer afternoons I rode into the Schleissheimer woods with a book on my handlebar. My supper I bought in a Schwabing provision shop, and washed it down with tea or beef extract.

I had close and sympathetic relations with Kurt Martens, the author of novels and short stories; he has vividly commemorated this friendship, in which he had taken the initiative, in his memoirs. He belonged to the few people—I could count them on the fingers of one hand—whom I ever addressed as "*du.*" The designer Markus Behmer visited me too, and was enthusiastic over my story *The Wardrobe*. Also Arthur Holitscher, for whose latest novel I had spoken at Langen's; we played music together. I read from *Buddenbrooks* to him and Martens. Holitscher, the aesthete and later communist, could find little that appealed to him in my bourgeois scribblings; but Martens showed an astonishing sympathy, for which I have always remained grateful. It was through him that I met Hans Weber, his cousin, editor and publisher of *Der Zwiebelfisch;* also Alfred Kubin, whose uncanny and obscene designs made a profound impression on me. Later on he made the grotesque and sombre cover for the first edition of *Tristan.*

I have left out of account the literary experiences of my childhood and early youth: the indelible impression Hans Christian Andersen's fairy stories made on me; the evenings when our mother read aloud out of Fritz Reuter's novel *Ut mine Stromtid,* or sang to us at the piano; my idolatry of Heine when I wrote my first poems; the enraptured hours after school when I sat snug with a whole plate of open sandwiches before me and read Schiller.

But I will not quite pass over the great and decisive impressions that came to me from my reading in the years at which I have now arrived. I mean the experience of Schopenhauer and Nietzsche. Probably my earliest prose writings that saw the light of print betray clearly enough the intellectual and stylistic influence of Nietzsche. In *The Reflections of a Non-Political Man* I have described my attitude of mind toward that whole compelling complex and traced it back to the personal factors that delimited and conditioned it. Certainly the contact with Nietzsche was to a high degree decisive for an intellect still in its formative stage; but to alter our very substance, to make something different out of us from what we are—that no cultural force is in a position to do; every possibility of cultural growth must presuppose an entity which possesses the instinctive will and capacity to make personal choices, to assimilate what it receives and work it over to suit its peculiar needs. Goethe says that to do something one must be something. But even to learn something, in any higher sense, one must be something. I leave to the critics to investigate—should they feel so inclined—what sort of modification, what sort of transmutation the art and ethos of Nietzsche suffered in my case. It was, at all events, a complicated sort; it held itself scornfully aloof from the fashionable and popular doctrines of Nietzscheism—the cult of the superman, the easy "Renaissancism," the Caesar Borgia aesthetics, all the blood- and beauty-mouthings then in vogue. The youth of twenty was clear upon the relativity of this great moralist's "immoralism." I watched the spectacle of his hatred for Christianity and, seeing beside it his brotherly love for Pascal, understood the hate in a moral but not a psychological sense—a distinction which I found to persist in Nietzsche's epochal war upon Wagner, that war upon what he loved best unto death. In a word, what I saw above all else in Nietzsche was the victor over self. I took nothing literally; I *believed* him hardly at all; and this precisely made my love for him a passion on two planes—gave it, in other words, its depth. Was I to take him seriously when he preached hedonism in art? When he played off Bizet against Wagner? What to me were his "blond beast" and his philosophy of force? Almost an embarrassment. His glorification of "life" at the expense of mind—that lyricism which turned out so disastrously for German thinking—I could assimilate in only one way: as self-criticism. True, the blond beast haunts my own youthful work; but it is, on the whole, divested of its bestial character, there is not much left of it but the blondness and the lack of mind—objects of that erotic irony and acceptance of the conservative, in which the mind, as it was quite well aware, did not give away too much. It did not matter that the transformation that Nietzsche suffered in me might almost be called making a bourgeois of him. It seemed to me then, and still seems today, profounder and shrewder than all the heroic-aesthetic paroxysms for which Nietzsche was responsible in literature. My Nietzsche experience was the prelude to a period of conservative thinking, from which I graduated at the time of the war; but it made me finally proof against the baleful romantic attraction which can—and today so often does—proceed from an *un*-human valuation of the relation between life and mind.

The whole experience, moreover, was not a matter of a single swift discovery and acceptance; it happened, as it were, in a series of thrusts extending over several years. Its earliest effect was a psychological susceptibility, a power of vision, a melancholy, which even today I hardly understand, but under which I had to suffer indescribably. Tonio Kröger says there is such a thing as being "sick of knowledge." The phrase describes quite accurately that sickness of my youth. If I remember rightly, it played a great part in making me receptive to the philosophy of Schopenhauer, to which I came only after some acquaintance with Nietzsche. *That* was a spiritual experience of absolutely first rank and unforgettable in kind— whereas the Nietzsche experience was more intellectual and artistic. With the volumes of Schopehauer it happened to me as I made it happen to Thomas Buddenbrook with the book he kept in the drawer of the garden table: I had bought the Brockhaus edition at a sale, more to own than to study it, and the volumes had stood a long time uncut on the shelves. But the hour came that bade me read, and I read day and night, as perhaps one reads only once in his life. To the fulness of my rapture it certainly contributed that this powerful intellectual and moral denial of life and the world was couched in a system of thought whose symphonic music appealed to my very depths. But mine was essentially a metaphysical intoxication, closely related to a late and violent outbreak of sexuality (I am speaking of my twentieth year) and in its nature less philosophical than passionate and mystical. I was not concerned with "wisdom," with the doctrine of salvation by conversion of the will—that ascetic-Buddhistic adjunct, the value of which to me was purely critical and polemic. What did concern me, and that in a sensual and suprasensual way, was the element of eroticism and mystic unity in this philosophy—an element that also had influenced the not in the least ascetic music of *Tristan*—and if in those days I was emotionally close to suicide, it was just because I had grasped the thought that it would be by no means an act of "wisdom." Ah, youth, with its sacred pangs, its urgency, its disorders! It was a happy chance that these supra-bourgeois experiences of mine came at a time when I could weave them into the close of my bour-

geois novel, where they served to prepare Thomas Buddenbrook for death.

The novel was finished at the turn of the century; I had
worked on it, off and on, for some two and a half years.
The manuscript went to Fischer, with whom, after *Little
Herr Friedemann*, I felt I had a connection. I still remember packing it; clumsily dropping the hot wax on my hand
and making a big blister which was to hurt for days. It was
an impossible manuscript, written on both sides. I had
meant to copy it, but this job got the upper hand of me and
I gave it up. Thus, the manuscript looked shorter than it
was, but on all counts was a harsh test for readers and type-
setters. There was but the one and only copy, so I registered it, and after the word "manuscript" on the wrapper
wrote down a value of one thousand marks. The post-
office clerk smiled.

The anxious consultations at Fischer's over my shape-
less offering took place while I was on military service. I
had "my year to serve." Once or twice I had been refused
on account of a narrow-chestedness or a "nervous heart,"

but now I looked well enough to deceive a staff doctor as to my fitness. I was accepted, reported at the infantry guard regiment, and had myself measured for a uniform.

I had lived in the barracks atmosphere for only a few weeks when my determination to free myself became deadly and, as it turned out, irresistible. I suffered tortures from the noise, the enforced idleness, the iron compulsion to be trim. And I acquired on parade march a severe, extremely painful inflammation of the sinew of the ankle. I went on the sick list, then into hospital; and when I had lain there two weeks with a potassium-silicate dressing it was too late for me to catch up with the training. Just as it had been at school. I went back to the barracks, and the inflammation returned at once, though less severely. It would serve my purpose. My mother's physician was acquainted with the ranking staff doctor. I was granted leave; at New Year's, three months after my induction, I was released. I signed—how joyfully!—a renunciation of all claims to compensation for my injury; and the commission that examined me afresh on this point assigned me to the category of "Last Reserve"—which amounted to final release. Never again have I had any personal connection with the army. Neither did the war lay hand on me physically, simply because the first doctor to whom I was taken had read my books; he laid his hand on my bare shoulder and declared: "You shall be left alone." The others later submitted to his verdict.

In the meantime the publishing house in Berlin had been troubled with doubts and scruples—apparently only too well justified—concerning my manuscript. But these were overcome—partly in consequence of a letter I sent to Fischer from the garrison hospital. I wrote in pencil, protesting against the suggestions to shorten the book, and declaring that its length was an essential characteristic, not to be laid hands on lightly. The letter, written and sent under the spur of strong feeling, did not fail of its effect. Fischer decided to publish, and *Buddenbrooks* came out at the end of 1900—with the imprint of 1901—in two yellow paper volumes costing six marks each.

Let no one suppose that the book went well from the start. The publisher's fears seemed about to be realized.

Nobody wanted to spend so much money on the unwieldy production of an obscure young author. The critics were put out: were triple-deckers coming again, they asked. They said my book was like a heavy dray grinding through sand. But other voices began to be lifted, among press and public. I pricked up my ears when I was congratulated by Carl Schüler, the proprietor of the Ackermann bookshop in the Maximilianstrasse. Schüler was a good friend from the time of the University Dramatic Club; he had heard, he said, that I had made a big hit. And Samuel Lublinski, an ailing Jewish critic, now deceased, wrote with singular decisiveness in the *Berliner Tageblatt* that the book would grow with the time and be read by generations yet to come. Nobody else went so far as that. However, in the course of the year the first printing of a thousand copies was sold out, and then the novel received the format in which it was to begin its astonishing career, a career as little foreseen by its author as by anybody else. Acting on advice from people who pointed to the record sales of Frenssen's *Jörn Uhl*, the publishing house got out the one-volume five-mark edition with Wilhelm Schulz's Biedermeier cover design; the press, even the foreign press, grew louder in its praise, and presently the printings began to tread on one another's heels.

It was fame. I was snatched up into a whirl of success, just as twice later in my life, within a few years: on the occasion of my fiftieth birthday, and again now, with the Nobel Prize award. Each time I have gone through it with mixed feelings, full of gratitude and incredulity. My mail was swollen, money flowed in streams, my picture appeared in the papers, a hundred pens made copy of the product of my secluded hours, the world embraced me amid congratulations and shouts of praise.

The moods and feelings of this time have many of them been embodied in the undramatic dramatic dialogues of *Fiorenza*. A failure as a finished product, though not without boldness in design, in five and twenty years it has not ceased to ruffle faintly the theatrical waters, and on occasion has floated upon them. Part of it is most personal and primordial: the youthful love of fame, the fear of fame, in one early involved in its toils: "O world! O deep delight. O love-dream of power, so sweet, consuming! One may not possess. Yearning is giant power, possession unmans."

Fiorenza came out in 1906. It was preceded by the

volume of short stories that contained *Tonio Kröger*—of all I have written perhaps still dearest to my heart today, and still beloved by the young.

I conceived the idea when I was working on *Buddenbrooks*, in the days of my activities at Langen's. I spent a two weeks' holiday in that excursion via Lübeck to Denmark which is described in the tale; and the impressions of my visit to Aalsgard am Sund, near Helsingör, were the nucleus round which the elements of the allusive little composition shot together. I wrote it very slowly. Particularly the middle part, lyric and prose essay in one, the conversation with the entirely imaginary Russian woman friend, cost me months. I remember that on one of my repeated sojourns at Riva on Lake Garda, in R. von Hartungen's "Haus zur Sonne," I had the manuscript with me without coming forward a single line. It is long since I saw the original sheets, but my memory of them is still vivid. I had at that time a curiously long-suffering technique: after finishing a work I would black out all the deletions with a thick cross-hatching of ink and by this means produce a clean copy of a sort. The cross-hatching must not be blotted, it had to dry; so in the last stage all the sheets were spread out over the floor and the furniture. The facsimile edition of *Tristan* shows this method.

Tonio Kröger appeared in 1903 in the *Neue Deutsche Rundschau*. It was warmly received by Berlin literary circles. It has the advantage of its bloom of youthful lyricism over *Death in Venice*, to which it is most nearly related; and, in a purely artistic sense, it may be that its musical qualities were what most endeared it to its readers. Here perhaps for the first time I learned to use music to mould my style and form. Here for the first time I grasped the idea of epic prose composition as a thought-texture woven of different themes, as a musically related complex—and later, in *The Magic Mountain*, I made use of it on a larger scale. It has been said of the latter work that it is an example of "the novel as architecture of ideas"; if that be true, the tendency toward such a conception goes back to *Tonio Kröger*. In particular, the linguistic leitmotif was not handled, as in *Buddenbrooks*, purely on an external and naturalistic basis, but was transferred to the more lucent realm of ideas and emotions, and thus lifted from the mechanical into the musical sphere.

.   .   .

The astounding triumphal progress of my family novel could not fail to alter the circumstances of my life. No longer was I the entirely obscure young man of former days. What I had been biding my time for, in my Schwabing and my Roman retreats, was now—I will not say attained, but entered upon. No longer did it embarrass me to be questioned about my daily life. No longer did anybody need to question—the facts were given in a Munich guidebook, a sort of Who's Who, wherein my address was set down as that of the author of *Buddenbrooks*. I had demonstrated my position, justified my flat resistance to the demands for regularity made upon me by the world; society took me up—in so far as I let it, for in this respect society has never been very successful. Still, I did begin to frequent a few Munich drawing rooms where there was an artistic and literary atmosphere: in particular that of the poetess Ernst Rosmer, the wife of the well-known lawyer Max Bernstein. And thence to the Pringsheim home in Arcisstrasse, a centre of social and artistic life in the Munich of Ludwig II and the Regency, the Lenbach decades —I had been present at the imposing funeral ceremonies of the latter.

The atmosphere of the Pringsheim home, that great family house that recalled my own early abode, enchanted me. I had known the traditional elegance that belonged to the great families; here I found it transformed and intellectualized in this stately society compact of art and literature. Each of the five grown children (they were five as we were, the two youngest twins) had his own beautifully bound library, quite separate from the rich collections of art and music books owned by the head of the house, one of the first Wagnerians, personally acquainted with the master. Only by a sort of intelligent self-compulsion did he devote himself to mathematics (he lectured at the University) instead of wholly to music. The lady of the house came of a Berlin literary family, being the daughter of Ernst and Hedwig Dohm. My existence and my youthful performance were not lost upon her, nor did she oppose the passionate feeling that soon grew up in me for the only daughter of the house—a feeling which my solitary youth had not taught me any need to dissimulate. There was a ball in the gilded High Renaissance salons of the Pringsheim house, a brilliant and numerous gathering, where for the first time I was conscious of basking in the full sunshine of public favour and regard; it ripened in me the feelings upon which I hoped to base the happiness of my life.

Once before, many years earlier, I had been close to matrimony. In a pension in Florence I had made friends with two of my tablemates, English sisters; the elder, who was dark, I found sympathetic, but the younger, who was blonde, delightful. Mary, or Molly, returned my feelings, there followed a tender relationship and talk of marriage. What held me back were certain misgivings: perhaps it was too soon to marry, perhaps the difference of nationality would be a bar. I think the little English girl felt the same; at any rate, the friendship came to nothing. This time everything was different. It may be that even inwardly I was on wooing bent; I was probably ready and anxious for marriage. All the circumstances favoured the event, and in February 1905, a man of thirty, I exchanged rings with my fairy bride.

Six children have come of the union: the eldest, Erika, now a member of the Munich Staatstheater, was born in 1906, and Michael, the youngest, in a time of danger, amid the thunder of cannon, on the day when the Communist republic had fallen and the "white" troops entered Munich. The next to the youngest, named Elisabeth after my father's mother, and now eleven years old, is nearest to my heart. She is the childish heroine of the little tale of the revolution and inflation period, called *Early Sorrow*—wherein the whimsical assertion of my cultural conservatism mingles with fatherly affection toward the new young world. It had a friendly reception in Germany and abroad. I wrote that story in 1925—immediately after finishing *The Magic Mountain*—for the number of *Die Neue Rundschau* which was dedicated to my fiftieth birthday.

The first fruit of my married state had been the novel *Royal Highness*, and it bears the marks of its origin. Here was an attempt to write a comedy in the form of a novel; it was likewise an attempt to come to terms, as a writer, with my own happiness. The result was generally criticized as being—after *Buddenbrooks*—too light. Certainly with justice. Yet both the imaginative intent and the scope of this fairy tale of real life did reach deeper than was generally perceived, and they were not quite without a groping and instinctive touch of prophecy. I am not speak-

ing of the analysis of the dynastic idea—which could probably not have been made in so sympathetic a vein if I had
not been dealing with an institution ripe for decay. But the
"happiness" that was the theme of *Royal Highness* was
not meant altogether banally and eudaemonistically. A
problem was here resolved under the guise of comedy, but
it was a problem nonetheless, one actually felt, not merely
idle. In this novel a young married man explored, by means
of a fable, the possibility of harmonizing the claims of
society and the solitary, of synthesizing form and life,
and of reconciling the melancholy consciousness of aris-
tocracy to the new demands which even then might have
been stated in the "democratic" formula. His whimsical
fancies, which had an appropriately autobiographical
stamp, deliberately omitted any tendentious or didactic
appeal; but I should like to think that the comedy had its
serious side and that some almost political foreshadowings
issued from it into the Germany of 1905.

We spent much time in the country in summer: in Ober-
ammergau, where I wrote most of *Royal Highness*, and

then a number of years in Tölz on the Isar, where we bought a house in 1908. It was in Tölz that death came home to our family for the first time since the passing of my father, and the loss shook me to my very depths, as that earlier one quite naturally had not been able to do. My second sister, Carla, took her own life. She had chosen a stage career, well equipped for it by her beauty but scarcely by any deeply rooted original gift. As a small child she had already been near death; a frightful complication of convulsions, whooping-cough, and inflammation of the lungs had made the doctors despair of her growing up. Her existence continued a frail and precarious one. A proud, disdainful nature, unconventional but refined, she loved literature, art, the manifestations of mind; and the crude unkindly time drove her into an unhappy bohemian existence. A taste for the macabre made her as a girl adorn her room with a death's head, to which she gave a scurrilous name; yet—the two things go very well together—she was as childishly laughter-loving as the rest of us. Later she kept poison by her—from what source we could only guess—and that too was probably a piece of playful fancy. I think, however, that the proud resolve was already present, not to suffer any degradation life might have in store for her. Without manifest talents of a literary or trainable kind, she seized passionately upon the theatre as a sphere of possible activity and self-realization. Not being what people call a "born actress," she tried to compensate for the lack of the essential gift by an artificial accentuation of her person and her femininity, so that one soon got the disquieting impression that a problem was being taken hold of by the wrong end, and with fatal lack of understanding. Her career came to a standstill in the provinces. Disappointed in her professional aspirations, she remained the object of desire. Apparently she tried to find a way back into the bourgeois sphere, and her hopes centred about a marriage with the young son of an Alsatian industrialist, who was in love with her. But she had before this given herself to another man, a doctor by profession, who used his power over her for his own gratification. The young fiancé found himself deceived and called her to account. Then she took her cyanide, enough to kill a whole company of soldiers.

The deed was done almost in the presence of our poor mother, at her country home in Polling, near Weilheim in Upper Bavaria, whither she, the once admired *grande dame*, had withdrawn with her furniture, her books and treasured possessions, and her increasing need of solitude and peace. My sister was on a visit to her, and the betrothed had made his appearance. Coming from an interview with him, the unhappy creature hurried past her mother with a smile, locked herself into her room, and the last that was heard from her was the sound of the gargling with which she tried to cool the burning of her corroded throat. She had time, after that, to lie down on the couch. Dark spots on the hands and face showed that death by suffocation— after a brief delay—must have ensued very suddenly. A note in French was found: *"Je t'aime. Une fois je t'ai trompé, mais je t'aime."* My wife and I were roused by a telephone call, the veiled language of which did not do much to hide the truth, and in the dawn I drove to Polling, to my mother's arms, to receive her moans upon my breast.

She never recovered from the blow thus dealt her aging, weak, and anxious heart. In mine, sorrow for our lost one, pity for all she must have suffered, mingled with reproaches for this awful deed committed almost in our fragile mother's sight, and with outrage against the deed itself. Its self-sufficiency, the stern and shockingly final life-and-death actuality of it seemed somehow like a betrayal of our brother-and-sisterly bond, a bond of destiny which I—it is hard to put into words—had ultimately regarded as objectively superior to the realities of life, and which, in my view, my sister's act showed her to have forgotten. In truth there was no justice in my grievance. For had not I too grown vastly "actual" by dint of work and dignities, wife and child and home and all the serious and humanly pleasant things of this life whatever they are called? And if in my case actuality wore a blithe and benignant face, still it was made of the same stuff as my sister's deed and involved the same breach of faith. All actuality is deadly earnest; and it is morality itself that, one with life, forbids us to be true to the guileless unrealism of our youth.

That was in 1910. My mother, her spirit more and more broken, survived her younger daughter for twelve years. Her last days fell in the period of the revolution, hunger, and inflation. She grew constantly more modest in her claims upon life, asking not even so much as befitted her station, and spent her time chiefly in bringing food from the country to supply her children's needs. The honours which her sons had earned filled her with childlike joy; any adverse word they had to put up with had to be sedulously hidden from her. At seventy she died, a gentle death after a slight illness; and so fate spared her another blow, the lamentable loss of her eldest daughter, Julia, named after her. The love that bore and nourished us seems to have better equipped the sons than the daughters for the struggle of life. For our two sisters both died by their own hand. With the fate of the second, seventeen years after the catastrophe at Polling, I am reluctant to deal here. Her grave is too new; I will leave the story to a later narrative in a larger frame.

On finishing *Royal Highness* I began to write the *Confessions of Felix Krull, Confidence Man*—a singular enterprise to which, as many people have guessed, I was led by reading the memoirs of Manolescu. Here, of course, was a new twist to the theme of art-and-the-artist, to the psychology of the unreal, the illusionary form of exist-

ence. But what intrigued me stylistically was the directness of the autobiographical form, which I had never
before tried, and which my rough-hewn model laid to my
hand. At the same time, a peculiar intellectual attraction
emanated from the burlesque idea of taking a much-loved
tradition—self-portraiture in the Goethe manner, the introspective confessions of the born aristocrat—and trans-
ferring it to the criminal sphere. The idea has really
great comic possibilities; and I so enjoyed writing the first
chapters—this torso was later published by the Deutsche
Verlags-Anstalt—that I was not surprised to hear from
people well qualified to judge that the fragment as it stands
is the happiest and best thing I have done. In a way it may
be the most personal, representing as it does my attitude
toward tradition, which is at once kindly and destructive,
and which determines my "mission" as a writer. The inner
laws that later produced *The Magic Mountain*—that epic
of a cultural development—were of the same nature.

It proved to be hard to sustain the right tone for the Krull
memoirs over any great length of time; and probably my

need for rest favoured the growth of the new idea by which they were presently—in the spring of 1911—interrupted. My wife and I—not for the first time in our lives—spent a part of May on the Lido. There a series of curious circumstances and impressions combined with my subconscious search for something new to give birth to a productive idea, which then developed into the story *Death in Venice*. The tale as at first conceived was as modest as all the rest of my undertakings: I thought of it as a quick improvisation which should serve as interlude to my work on the Krull novel; in material and scope it was to be something that might do for *Simplicissimus*. But things—or whatever better word there may be for the conception *organic*—have a will of their own, and shape themselves accordingly: for instance, *Buddenbrooks*, planned with A. L. Kielland for a model, as a novel of merchant life, perhaps some two hundred and fifty pages long, had its own way with me; *The Magic Mountain* was to do the same; and Aschenbach's story proved perverse in more than the sense I had planned for it.

The truth is that every piece of work is a realization, fragmentary but complete in itself, of our individuality;

and this kind of realization is the sole and painful way we have of getting the particular experience—no wonder, then, that the process is attended by surprises! Here—I borrow the figure from crystallography, since it is so apt —many elements shot together to produce an image which, playing in the light of its many facets, floating in the aura of its manifold associations, might well cause the eye of one watching and conspiring at its development to lose itself in a dream. I love that word *associations*. For me, and in however relative a sense, that which is full of associations is, quite precisely, that which is significant. How well I remember my feeling of grateful acknowledgement when Ernst Bertram read aloud to us from the manuscript the profound Venetian chapter of his Nietzsche mythology and I heard him utter the name of my little tale!

As inwardly, so outwardly, all the elements of the fable fell into the picture in the most singular way. I was reminded of my experience with *Tonio Kröger* by the inherent symbolism and rightness for composition of even the most unimportant of the factual elements. In that tale of my youth one might suppose that the scenes in the library or with the police officer were invented to make my point. They were not; they are quite simply taken from the facts. In the same way, nothing is invented in *Death in Venice*. The "pilgrim" at the North Cemetery, the dreary Pola boat, the gray-haired rake, the sinister gondolier, Tadzio and his family, the journey interrupted by a mistake about the luggage, the cholera, the upright clerk in the travel bureau, the rascally ballad-singer, all that, and anything else you like, they were all there; I had only to arrange them, when they showed at once and in the oddest way their capacity as elements of composition. Perhaps it had to do with this: that as I worked on the story—as always, it was a long-drawn-out job—I had at moments the clearest feeling of transcendence, a sovereign sense of being borne up, such as I had never before experienced. I was living at the time alone with the children at Tölz— for reasons about to be explained—and the sympathy and enthusiasm of the friends to whom I read the story aloud in the evenings in my little study might have prepared me for the almost stormy reception it was to have on its publication. The German public really only likes serious and significant stuff; it does not care for light reading: and, despite its questionable subject, the book was taken as a sort of moral rehabilitation of the author of *Royal High-ness*. In France the "*petit roman*" was very well received. Edmond Jaloux wrote a spirited foreword to the transla-tion.

In 1912 my wife had been attacked by a catarrh of the tip of the lung. Then, and again in the next year but one, she was obliged to stay for several months in the Swiss Alps. In May and June of 1912 I spent three weeks with her in Davos, and accumulated—the word but ill describes the extreme passivity of my state—the fantastic impressions out of which the Hörselberg idea shaped itself into a short tale. I distinctly thought of it as another brief interlude to the *Confessions*, which were still luring me on, and as a satyr play to the tragic novella of decay just finished. The fascination of death, the triumph of extreme disorder over a life founded upon order and consecrated to it—these were to be reduced in scale and dignity by a humorous treatment. A simple-minded hero, a droll conflict between macabre adventure and bourgeois sense of duty—the out-come was not decided but would surely be found, and the whole be easy and amusing and not take much space. When I came back to Tölz and Munich I began to write the first chapter of *The Magic Mountain*, and even read bits of it aloud in the Galerie Caspari—Wedekind, I remember, was there.

At bottom I hardly concealed from myself the possibilities for expansion, the propensities of my material. I was early conscious that it belonged to a dangerous concentration of "associations." I shall never fathom—and should do better not to try—why every working idea of mine presents itself to me in a harmless, simple, practicable light, as involving no great effort in the execution. But certainly, to envisage too clearly beforehand all the difficulties of a task, and its claims on one's time and strength, would be enough to make one shudder and forgo it. Just this is prevented by an apparatus of self-deception, which probably functions somewhat in response to appeals from the conscious self. I was early aware that the Davos story "had something to it"; that it "thought of itself" quite differently from the way I had to think in order to embark upon it. Outwardly, even, it gave notice: the comfortable English key I began in—as it were, by way of resting from the rigours of *Death in Venice*—the expansive humour simply demanded room. Also *The Magic Mountain* profited—in respect of form—by the war, which drove me to a general revision of my principles, to the painful and conscientious searchings exhibited in *The Reflections of a Non-Political Man;* by dint of which the worst of the introspective burden was lifted from the novel—or rather they helped to ripen it for composition. But the problems dealt with in the narrative, like those in the volume of confession and struggle, were all present and alive in me before the war; everything was there before the war—it was only actualized, and bathed in the lurid and desolate light of the conflagration.

The nerve-racking days before the mobilization, the outbreak of the international catastrophe, we spent in our retreat in Tölz. But we got an idea of how things stood in the country and in the world when we drove into town to take leave of my youngest brother, who was in the artillery reserve and left at once for the front. We saw the hot August hurly-burly of the railroad stations, choked with a host of distracted humanity shaken and torn by anguish and enthusiasm. The fatality took its course. I shared to the full the pangs of intellectual Germany in the clutch of destiny; which had faith in so much that was true and so much that was false, so much that was right and so much that was wrong, and which was marching to meet such frightful experiences—frightful and yet, taken all in all, wholesome and furthering its maturity and growth. I trod this path together with my nation, the stages of my experience were theirs, and as such do I accept it. But while on the one hand there was nothing in my tastes or cultural traditions—which were moral and metaphysical, not political and social—to hold me aloof, as others were held, perhaps only too naturally; yet on the other I knew myself, in my physical essence, not made for a soldier and a fighting man. For no more than a moment, in the beginning, was I tempted to disclaim this knowledge. "To suffer with you"—for that there was ample opportunity in the years that followed, in both the physical and the mental sphere; and the *Reflections of a Non-Political Man* was a war service with the weapon of thought, for which, as I

have said in the Foreword, the time, rather than country
or army, enlisted me.

With the actual army I came into contact only once
during the war. It was in occupied Brussels, and I had an
adventurous drive thither, being invited to a performance
of *Fiorenza* given by the German dramatic company in
the Théâtre Royal du Parc. I breakfasted with the com-
mandant of the town, the Bavarian General Hurt, surrounded by his officers, all dapper and affable people, and
one and all, for what service I know not, decorated with
the Iron Cross First Class. One of them—he had been a
chamberlain at a Thuringian court—later addressed me
in a letter as Herr Comrade-in-Arms; and really the vicis-
situdes of the war hit me as hard as they did these
people.

In January 1914, while my wife was still at Arosa, I had
moved with the children into the home we had built for
ourselves in the Bogenhausen quarter on the Isar. And
here we lived through the years of horror and wretched-
ness; we saw the ruin and the catastrophe, the failure of an
undoubtedly genuine if politically ill-advised and histori-
cally false uprising; we felt the revolting and unnerving

CARL A. RUDISILL LIBRARY
LENOIR RHYNE COLLEGE

sense of being delivered over to foreigners and had the disorders of domestic dissolution break upon us.

The feeling had been strong in me from the beginning that here was the epochal turning-point of an age, whose profound meaning for me personally could not be denied. This was the basis of that intoxication with fate which gave my attitude toward the war its positively German character. To pursue the tasks I had in hand was not to be thought of—or, rather, after repeated trials, proved mentally impossible. Out of a stock of material that had been accumulating for years I hastily vamped up the essay *Frederick the Great and the Grand Coalition*—its realistic delineation of the king doggedly gave notice that my faculty of polemic essay-writing remained on the alert. And then, by dint of repeated attacks, began my work on the *Reflections*—a thrashing through the pathless underbrush which was to go on for two years. I have never done any work that seemed so private to myself, so utterly without public implications. I was alone with my torment. To no one who enquired could I even make it clear what I was about. Ernst Bertram was the confidant of my endless political-anti-political introspections. I read aloud to him from them when he was in Munich; he respected them as a passionate, imperative searching of the conscience, and was at home in their Protestantism and conservatism. As far as this last goes, I know precisely that I felt it more as an artistic inquest and conquest of the melancholic-reactionary sphere than as an ultimate expression of my being. It was a psychological—or, if you like, in the literal sense, a pathological—phenomenon: what I thought stood in the sign and under the seal of the war, and spoke for itself more than for me. And yet there reigned the most painful solidarity and unity between the writer and this subject of his that was so difficult of precise definition. The problem of the German nation there treated was beyond a doubt my own—therein lay the national character of the book, which through all the torment, all the polemical perversity proved at last its *raison d'être* as an educational document. "*Que diable allait-il faire, dans cette galère?*" That was its fitting motto, as also the line of *Tasso* that headed it: "*Vergleiche dich, erkenne was du bist!*" I should have added a third, if I had found it sooner: "No one remains precisely what he is, when he knows himself."

The *Reflections* appeared in 1918, at what, to outward

appearance, was the most unfavourable, indeed, the most impossible of moments: the time of the collapse and the revolution. But in reality it was the right moment. The tasks, the intellectual necessities which the German *bourgeoisie* had now to face, I had gone through earlier, and had spoken out; many found it helpful—in fact, I like to think that the book has its meaning and value for the history of culture; not only the value of steadfastness but in its character as the last great retreat action, fought not without gallantry, of a romantic *bourgeoisie* in face of the triumphant "new."

An animal story, called *A Man and His Dog*, which, thanks to a capital translation, was particularly well received in England, and a somewhat eccentric experiment with an idyll in hexameters, *Gesang vom Kindchen*, which later, under more favourable circumstances, was superseded and improved on by *Early Sorrow*—these two formed the transition to a new period of creative activity. I took up *The Magic Mountain* again; but the work upon it was accompanied by the composition of critical essays of which the three most important in their scope were immediate offshoots from the novel. These were *Goethe and*

Tolstoy, The German Republic, and *An Experience in the Occult.* I shall probably never be able to protect my creative work, however much more rewarding it is to me, from being interrupted or prolonged in the most annoying way by my tendency to essay, or even to polemical, writing. This tendency goes back a long way and is obviously an indefeasible element of my personality. Perhaps in yielding to it I am more aware of sharing Goethe's consciousness of being "a born writer" than when I am spinning a tale. That is why I do not care for the popular distinction we make in Germany between a creative author and a writer. Surely the line between the two does not run outwardly between the manifestations, but within the personality, and even there is entirely fluid. "An art," as I said in my Lessing address in 1928, "whose medium is language will always exhibit a high degree of critical creativeness, for language itself is a criticism of life: it names, it defines, it hits the mark, it passes judgment, and all by making things alive." And yet, shall I confess that I regularly find mere "writing," as distinct from the free composition of the creative author, a sort of passionate truancy and a self-tormenting theft from happier tasks? There is much sense of duty, a smack of the categorical imperative in play here, and one might comment on the paradox of asceticism with a bad conscience, if it were not that a good deal of pleasure and satisfaction are bound up with it—as is the case with all asceticism. In any case, my essay-writing proclivities seem fated to accompany and act as critique upon my creative work. *Buddenbrooks* is my only considerable work which was not interrupted by essay-writing; but an essay followed it: *Bilse und ich*, an argumentation in the form of an enquiry into the relation between the writer and reality. This from 1906; in 1910 there appeared two considerable essays: one *Versuch über das Theater*, to the theme of which I returned at the Heidelberg Festival, and *The Old Fontane*, which I like best of all my digressions in this kind. Indeed, after the war, in a time tortured by problems, a time when it was hard to collect one's thoughts, there was no lack of demands upon me from the outer world; and the author of *Reflections* had the least of all his like the right to refuse them. Thus, inner compulsion united with the needs of the time to produce the addresses, discussions, introductions, rejoinders, which eventually filled three volumes. Of these the speeches beginning with *The German Republic* which I gave in the winter of 1922–3 in the Beethoven-Saal in Berlin represent, above and beyond the literary, elevated moments in my personal life.

I may recall here one happy theatrical experience, which fell to my lot in Vienna soon after the war: a performance of *Fiorenza* for ever memorable because it was given under such favourable circumstances that for the first time I felt none of the pangs of conscience that usually assail the author on such occasions. Dr. Wilhelm Rosenthal, then Director of the Volkstheater, was a lover of this work of mine. He had entrusted its performance to a dramatic company selected from the Burg- and the Volkstheater so that even the smallest rôles were interpreted by artists who were arresting personalities and masters of diction. It was given in the Akademietheater, with its ample stage and intimate auditorium, the latter filled with a warmly disposed and international audience. I sat in a box near the stage, and my own lively interest astonished me. The historical situation came to the aid of my youthful production, of whose weaknesses and double nature I was at all times only too conscious, and helped to make it effective even in the eyes of the author himself. The decline of an aesthetic epoch and the rise of a society of suffering, the triumph of the religious over the cultural—there was a general receptivity for such themes, and the evening was memorable in that it gave me food for thought upon the existence of a sensitiveness—not of any very agitating kind, of course, something that would only register itself, so to speak, on a seismograph—that seemed to me a form of political experience—only different, more subdued and indirect.

Meanwhile the enemy and neutral frontiers had opened; amid the smoke wreaths of the late conflagration a new Europe began to appear: reduced, as it were, in size, condensed, more intimate. Foreign lecture tours began, first to Holland, Switzerland, and Denmark, in the capital of which latter country I was the guest of the German ambassador and philosophic writer Gerhart von Mutius. In the spring of 1923 came a voyage to Spain undertaken by water in the still necessary avoidance of France: from Genoa to Barcelona, Madrid, Seville, and Granada, then back across the peninsula to Santander in the north, through the Bay of Biscay and via Plymouth to Hamburg. I shall not soon forget Ascension Day in Seville, the mass in the cathedral, the glorious organ music, and the gala *corrida* in the afternoon. But, on the whole, Andalusia and the south appealed to me less than the classic Spanish domain, Castile, Toledo, Aranjuez, Philip's granite fortress, and the drive past the Escorial to Segovia beyond the snow-topped Guadarrama. We just touched the English coast on the way home.

The year following I was the guest of the newly founded PEN Club in London, welcomed by Galsworthy in a cordial speech at the banquet, and the object of the clearest manifestations of a desire for intellectual reconciliation. Not until two years later was the way open for the visit to Paris, arranged by the French office of the Carnegie Foundation. I have recorded this visit in the little book *Pariser Rechenschaft*. The year 1927 brought a visit to Warsaw, where society welcomed the German writer with an unforgettable gesture of high-hearted hospitality and readiness to be friendly. I say *society* advisedly; for not only the closed circle of the PEN Club—which for the space of a week exhausted itself in attentions—but also nobility and officialdom united to give me the impression that there prevailed a sincere respect and gratitude for German culture, which seized upon this occasion to assert itself against political difficulties and antinomies.

It was in 1924, after endless intermissions and difficulties, that there finally appeared the book which, all in all, had had me in its power not seven but twelve years. Its reception would have needed to be much more unfavourable than it was, to surpass my expectations.

It is my way, when I have finished a book, to let it fall with a resigned shrug and not the faintest confidence in its chances in the world. The attraction it exerted upon me, its sponsor, has long since vanished; that I have finished it at all is a feat due to my convictions on the ethics of craftsmanship—due indeed, at bottom, to obstinacy. Altogether, obstinacy seems to me to have played such a part in these crabbed years-long preoccupations, I regard them so much as a highly dubious private enjoyment, that I question the likelihood of anyone caring to follow on the track of my curious morning occupations. My surprise is the greater when, as it has happened to me many times, the results are welcomed by an almost turbulent following.

In the case of *The Magic Mountain* my astonishment was particularly profound. Would anyone expect that a harassed public, economically oppressed, would take it on itself to pursue through twelve hundred pages the dream-like ramifications of this figment of thought? (*"Seines Liedes Riesenteppich, zweimalhunderttausend Verse"*—Heine's phrase from *Firdusi* had been my pet quotation throughout those twelve years, and also Goethe's *"Daß du nicht enden kannst, das macht dich groß."*) Would, under the circumstances then prevailing, more than a few thousand people be found willing to spend sixteen or twenty marks on such odd entertainment, which had really little or nothing in common with a novel in the usual sense of the word? Certain it is that ten years earlier the book would not have found readers—nor could it have been written. It needed the experiences which the author had shared with his countrymen; these he had to ripen within him in his own good time, and then, at the favourable moment, as once before, to come forward with his bold production. The subject matter of *The Magic Mountain* was not by its nature suitable for the masses. But with the bulk of the educated classes these were burning questions, and the national crisis had produced in the general public precisely that alchemical "keying-up" of which the actual adventure of little Hans Castorp had consisted. Yes, certainly the German reader recognized himself in the simple-minded but shrewd young hero of the novel. He could and would be guided by him.

I do not deceive myself as to the nature of this curious success. It was less epic than that of my youthful novel, more conditioned by the times, but not for that reason shallower or more ephemeral, for it rested upon a community of suffering. Success came more quickly than in the case of *Buddenbrooks:* the first newspaper notices sounded the alarm, the obstacle of the price was taken by assault, and it required only four years to bring the book to the hundredth printing. A Hungarian translation came out almost simultaneously with the original, the Dutch, English, and Swedish followed, and now, contrary to all the traditions of the Paris book trade, a French edition in two volumes, unabridged, is arranged for, and I have the happiest auguries of its reception in a moved and moving letter from André Gide, in which he writes of his weeks-long preoccupation with the book. I am convinced of the rightness of that fine phrase of Emile Faguet: *"L'étranger, cette postérité contemporaine."*

I have mentioned several times the playful little tale, *Early Sorrow*, which in 1925 followed the novel and in which I paid a sort of indulgent homage to disorder; but in truth I love order, love it as nature, as a profoundly legitimate necessity, as the inner fitness and clear correspondence of a productive plan of life. Thus, I take pleasure in seeing how in mine the two long novels are related to the two principal novellas, and these again to each other: *Tonio Kröger* corresponding to *Buddenbrooks* and *Death in Venice* to *The Magic Mountain;* and again the latter forming the creative pendant to the novel of my early days in precisely the same way that the Venetian study of decay does to the tale of youth under northern skies. Not before

I was fifty did *The Magic Mountain* consent to leave off; but it did not fail the day so bound up with a host of affecting and grateful memories of the friendliness of the German public.

In the following year the Prussian Minister of Education, Dr. Becker, founded the literary section of the Berlin Academy of the Arts and Letters, and I was appointed to the little group of electors. There was a full-dress meeting of the whole Academy, under the presidency of Liebermann—which got itself much talked about on account of Arno Holz's not very apropos hostility. I was chosen in the name of the section to thank the Minister for his speech of introduction and welcome; and I did not let slip the opportunity to refer to that antagonism to academic thought which exists in the German intellectual sphere, and to indicate the possibility of obviating it. I took the occasion to put the case of "the other side"—from the viewpoint of society as a whole; and this I did in the sincere conviction that here were the fitting time and place to carry out my resolve and speak. The official recognition of literature as an organ of the national life, its correlation, not to say its "elevation," into the official, was a logical consequence of Germany's social and national development, and no more than the confirmation of existing facts. It was not chance that I had been asked to speak; as perhaps no other, I had suffered in my own person, with whatever violent struggles, the compulsion of the times, which forced us out of the metaphysical and individual stage into the social; I too knew well the intellectual arguments with which many a German writer supported his own refusal; but it was my conviction that the writer must with the courage born of good will rise above his own self-conscious objections and the popular sneers, which were fundamentally cheap and reactionary; and this conviction of mine also had its history. It was my hope that the creative writer would perceive at last the task of reconciling —even in a decorative sense—the irreconcilable; of marrying the daemonic with the formal, the private and Bohemian with the official and representational, and feel their vital and mysterious fascination.

At about this time or earlier, a Munich artist, an old friend of my wife, showed me a portfolio of illustrations of his, depicting quite prettily the story of Joseph the son of Jacob. The artist wanted me to give him a word or so of introduction to his work, and it was partly in the mind to do him this friendly service that I looked up in my old family Bible—with its many underlinings in faded ink bearing witness to the study of long-dead pious forebears —the graceful fable of which Goethe said: "This natural narrative is most charming, only it seems too short, and one feels inclined to put in the detail." I did not know then how much the phrase, out of *Dichtung und Wahrheit*, was to mean to me as a motto in the years of work before me. But the evening hour was full of meditation, of tentative, groping speculation and the forecast of an entirely new thing; I felt an indescribable fascination of the mind and the senses at this idea of leaving the modern bourgeois sphere so far behind and making my narrative pierce deep, deep into the human. The tendencies of the time, the tastes of my own age united to make the theme alluring to me. The problem of man, thanks to the advance of his experimentations upon himself, has attained a peculiar actuality: the search for his essence, his origin, his goal, evokes everywhere a new humane interest and sympathy—I am using the word *humane* in its most scientific, objective sense, without any sentimental bearing. We have pushed forward our knowledge, whether into the darkness of prehistoric times or into the night of the unconscious; researches that at a certain point meet and fall together have mightily broadened the scope of our anthropological knowledge, back into the depths of time, or—what is really the same thing—down into the depths of the soul; and in all of us there is awake a lively curiosity about what is earliest and oldest in human things: the mythical, the legendary, the time before the dawn of reason. And these interests of today are not inappropriate tastes for a time of life that may legitimately begin to divorce itself from the peculiar and individual and turn its gaze upon the typical—which is, after all, the mythical. I do not say that the conquest of the myth, from the stage of development at which we have now arrived, can ever mean a mental return to it. That can happen only as a result of self-delusion. The ultra-romantic denial of the development of the cerebrum, the exorcizing of mind, which seems to be the philosophical order of the day, is not everybody's affair. To blend reason and sympathy in a gentle irony—that need not be profane: a technique, an inner atmosphere of some such kind would probably be the right one to incubate the problem I had in mind. Myth and psychology—the anti-intellectual bigots would prefer to have these two kept far apart. And yet, I thought, it might be amusing to attempt, by means of a mythical psychology, a psychology of the myth.

The fascination grew. It was strengthened by another thought: the idea of assimilation, of continuation, continuity, of contributing to human tradition—again an idea which gains in power of attraction at the age which I have now reached. The material belonged to an ancient, primeval realm of civilization and fancy; it was a favourite subject of all the arts, hundreds of times elaborated in the East and the West in picture and poesy. My work, for good or ill, would take its historic place in the line, in the tradition, bearing the stamp of its own time and place. The most important, the decisive thing is legitimacy. These dreams had their roots far back in my childhood. When I began to substantiate them upon archaeological and Oriental study I was only going back to a reading beloved in youth and an early passion for the land of the pyramids—childish conquests which had once in the fifth form made me confuse a teacher who had asked me the name of the sacred bull of the Egyptians and was answered with the original instead of the Graecized form of the name.

What I had in mind, of course, was a novella which should serve as one wing to a historical triptych, the other two dealing with Spanish and German subjects, the religious-historical theme running through the whole. The old story! Hardly had I begun to write—after long hesitation, long walking round and round the uncommonly hot porridge—when I found that I could no longer conceal even from myself the spacious claims to independence which the narrative set up. For my epic-writing pedantry, my mania for treatment *ab ovo* had made me take into my narrative the early and ancestral history; in particular, the figure of Jacob the father took up such a commanding position that the title *Joseph and His Brothers*, to which, on traditional grounds, I have clung, seems likely to end by becoming inadequate and giving place to another: *Jacob and His Sons*.

The difficulty is not a pressing one. I seem to have got about halfway with my tale at present (though that, to quote Hegel, may be "a trick of the reason"); and a few stylistic samples have been published in the *Neue Rund-schau* and *Die Literarische Welt*. But I was obliged to foresee that the work would not proceed without the usual delays and intervals of rest. Actually, a good part of the volume entitled *Die Forderung des Tages* consists of such interludes, in particular the careful study of Kleist's beloved *Amphitryon*, a work of critical homage, which, as we have no German Saint-Beuve, was pretty much without a model. In my young days I owed everything to models: without constant contact with admired examples I scarcely ventured on a single step; and yet with time I have come to feel that the whole essence of art is in their deliberate abandonment, in the leap in the dark, the possibility of achieving the *new;* no praise do I value higher than André Gide's when he wrote, about *The Magic Mountain: "Cette œuvre considérable n'est vraiment* comparable à rien."

The weeks of loving preoccupation with Kleist's comedy and the wonder of his metaphysical brilliance I will not call a waste of time, as all sorts of subterranean associations connected this critical task with my "main business"; and love is never uneconomical. But yet it pleases

me that among the impromptu occupations to which the
long narrative had to give way, there is one independent
tale, *Mario and the Magician*—and seldom, I suppose, has
any organic thing owed its origin to a more mechanical
set of circumstances.

As a family unanimously bent on letting no summer pass
without a stay at the seashore, my wife and I, with the
youngest children, spent August 1929 in Samland, in the
Baltic seaside resort of Rauschen, a choice conditioned by
appeals from East Prussia and particularly an oft-renewed
invitation from the Königsberg Goethe Society. It was
not feasible to take the swollen bulk of my uncopied manuscript of *Joseph* upon this extended though easy trip. But
I have no talent for unoccupied recreation, it is always sure
to do me more harm than good; so I resolved to spend my
mornings on the easy task of writing out an incident of a
previous holiday in Forte dei Marmi, near Viareggio, and
the impressions of our stay there; in other words, with a
piece of work which needed no apparatus but could be
written "straight out of my head" in the easiest possible
way. At my usual hour I began writing in my room, but
the feeling that the sea was waiting for me outside proved

not very conducive to work. I did not think I should be able to work out-of-doors. I must have, it seemed to me, a roof over my head, or my ideas would dissolve into thin air. This was a dilemma. Only the sea could produce it, but happily the sea proved able also to solve it. I let myself be persuaded to move my writing to the beach, drew my wicker chair down to the water's edge, which was crowded with bathers. While in the midst of this holiday bustle I sat with a pad on my knee and had before me the open sea constantly cut across by passers-by, and while children were picking up my pencils, the fable, all unexpectedly, grew out of the anecdote, the intellectualized literary form out of mere "story-telling"; the personal turned into the symbolic and ethical. And all the while I was in a state of joyful wonder, seeing how the sea had the power of absorbing human distractions and resolving them all in its loved immensity.

Our holidays had a practical over and above the literary result. We visited the Kurische Nehrung, whose landscape had often been recommended to us—it can boast that no less a person than Wilhelm von Humboldt has sung its praises—and spent a few days in the fishing village of

Nidden in Lithuanian Memelland. We were so thrilled by the indescribable and unique beauty of nature in this place —the fantastic world of sandy dunes mile on mile, the birch and pine groves full of elk between The Haff and the Baltic, the wild splendour of the beach—that we decided to acquire a dwelling-place in this remote spot, a pendant, as it were, to our South German home. We took the first steps, leased a strip of dune with a view of idyllic beauty and grandeur from the Lithuanian Forest Administration, and commissioned a firm of Memel architects. The little house has already had its thatch put on. Each year we shall spend in it the summer holidays of our school children.

The year was not to close without agitating events. The famous award of the Swedish Academy, which once more, after a space of seventeen years, fell to Germany's lot, had, I knew, hovered over me more than once before and found me not unprepared. It lay, I suppose, upon my path in life—I say this without presumption, with calm if not uninterested insight into the character of my destiny, of my "*rôle*" on this earth, which has now been gilded with

the equivocal brilliance of success; and which I regard
entirely in a human spirit, without any great mental ex-
citement. And just so, in such a spirit of reflective and
receptive calm, I have accepted as my lot in life the re-
sounding episode, with all its festal and friendly accom-
paniments, and gone through it with the best grace I could
muster—even inwardly, which is a harder matter. With
some imaginative yieldingness in their direction one might
derive the most priceless thrills from the experience of
being taken up, solemnly and with all the world looking
on, into the circle of immortals, of being able to call
Mommsen and France and Hauptmann and Hamsun
one's peers; but it is quenching to one's dreamy exaltation
to reflect upon those who have *not* got the prize. Moreover, it is clear, being so stated in the beautifully exe-
cuted document which King Gustav gave me, that I owe
the award primarily to the affection of the Northern people for my youthful novel of family life in Lübeck. And I
have to smile as I remember how consciously I laboured
to bring out the atmospheric similarity of my own and the
Scandinavian scene, in order to approximate my work to
that of my literary ideals. Even so, the Nobel Prize Com-

mittee would have scarcely been in a position to award me the prize without any of the other things which I have done since. If I had qualified for it only and already with *Buddenbrooks*, then why did I not receive it twenty-five years ago? The earliest indication I had that my name was being mentioned in this connection came to me in 1913, after the appearance of *Death in Venice*. Beyond a doubt the Committee comes quite freely to its own decisions; and yet it cannot, after all, follow only its own judgement. It must address itself to the approbation of the world in general; and I think that after *Buddenbrooks* something else had to come out of me before the Committee could count on even the degree of approbation that it did get.

The Stockholm event lent festal emphasis to a long-arranged-for lecture tour on the Rhine. The ceremonies in the Aula of the University of Bonn—whose Philosophical Faculty had conferred upon me the degree of *doctor honoris causa* shortly after the war—will remain ever memorable to me by reason of a press of students who subjected the ancient flooring to a serious test—so I was told by some worried professors. But it was unfortunate for the tour as a whole that it fell almost immediately before the journey north which made such large demands upon my strength—truly a journey which I must gratefully acknowledge to have been the friendliest, the most impressive I have ever known. I am not speaking of the stately brilliance of the actual ceremonies, when king and court rose with the audience—an extraordinary gesture— to honour the entering recipients of the prize. But whoever goes to Sweden as a representative of Germany, in whatever capacity he goes, will be well treated there. He is in the foreign country most friendly to Germany—a fact of which my toast at the banquet after the ceremonies made me abundantly aware; it moves me even now to recall the emotional sympathy with which every word was followed that I devoted to the pregnant destinies of my country and its people. And personally these festal days enriched my life with the human value of several new acquaintances: the wise and benign Archbishop Nathan Söderblom of Upsala; the charming Prince Eugen, who has painted the beautiful frescoes in the new City Hall; Selma Lagerlöf; Bonnier, the publisher; Hans von Euler-Chelpin, the Nobel Prize winner for chemistry; and Frederik Böök, academician and literary historian.

. . .

Only slowly after my return home did the waves begin to subside, after the flood tide upon which my life had risen. It is an unnerving experience to have come very publicly into the possession of a sum of money—as much as many an industrialist puts away every year and no notice taken of it—and suddenly to be stared in the face by all the misery in the world, which the amount of the figure has stimulated to assail the unlucky winner's conscience with claims of every size and kind. There was something indescribably menacing and even spitefully daemonic in the tone of the demand, in the expression of that thousand-headed need that reached out to clutch at the much-talked-of money. One saw oneself driven to a choice of two *rôles:* either the mammon-calloused wretch or the simpleton who flings into a bottomless well a sum of money intended for other ends. I cannot say that my organizing capacities were equal to the demands which my outer life put upon them in slowly and steadily mounting degree. To satisfy them would have needed a well-staffed office with departments for translation, book and manuscript criticism, charity, advice—in short, an organization which might hold at bay the consciousness of one's total inadequacy to the situation. Here again I do not know how to thank enough the wife who now for five and twenty years has shared my life—this difficult, so easily tired and distracted life, which asks, above all, for so much patience; I do not know how, without the wise, courageous, delicate yet energetic assistance of my incomparable companion and friend, I should sustain it even as well as I do.

Our wedding anniversary is near at hand, brought round by a year which is a round number, like all those that have been important in my life. It was midday when I came into the world; my fifty years lay in the middle of the decades, and in the middle of a decade, halfway through it, I was married. This pleases my sense of mathematical clarity, as does also the fact that my children come and go, as it were, in rhymed couples: girl, boy, boy, girl, girl, boy. I have a feeling that I shall die, at the same age as my mother, in 1945.

In the meantime we are preparing for a voyage to the scenes of my novel, Egypt and Palestine. I expect to find the sky above and much of the earth beneath unchanged after three thousand five hundred years.

The PRINCIPAL WORKS of THOMAS MANN

First Editions in German

DER KLEINE HERR FRIEDEMANN
[Little Herr Friedemann]. Tales

Berlin, S. Fischer Verlag.　1898

BUDDENBROOKS
Novel　　　　　　　　　　Berlin, S. Fischer Verlag.　1901

TRISTAN
Contains *Tonio Kröger*. Tales　Berlin, S. Fischer Verlag.　1903

FIORENZA
Drama　　　　　　　　　　Berlin, S. Fischer Verlag.　1905

KÖNIGLICHE HOHEIT
[Royal Highness]. Novel　　Berlin, S. Fischer Verlag.　1909

DER TOD IN VENEDIG
[Death in Venice]. Short novel

Berlin, S. Fischer Verlag.　1913

DAS WUNDERKIND
[The Infant Prodigy]. Tales　Berlin, S. Fischer Verlag.　1914

BETRACHTUNGEN EINES UNPOLITISCHEN
Autobiographical reflections　Berlin, S. Fischer Verlag.　1918

HERR UND HUND
[A Man and His Dog]. Idyll
Contains also *Gesang vom Kindchen,* an idyll in verse
Berlin, S. Fischer Verlag. 1919

WÄLSUNGENBLUT
Tale *München, Phantasus Verlag.* 1921

BEMÜHUNGEN
Essays *Berlin, S. Fischer Verlag.* 1922

REDE UND ANTWORT
Essays *Berlin, S. Fischer Verlag.* 1922

BEKENNTNISSE DES HOCHSTAPLERS FELIX KRULL: Buch der
Kindheit
Fragment of a novel
Stuttgart, Deutsche Verlags-Anstalt. 1923

DER ZAUBERBERG
[The Magic Mountain]. Novel
Berlin, S. Fischer Verlag. 1924

UNORDNUNG UND FRÜHES LEID
[Disorder and Early Sorrow]. Short novel
Berlin, S. Fischer Verlag. 1926

KINO
Fragment of a novel *Berlin, S. Fischer Verlag.* 1926

PARISER RECHENSCHAFT
Travelogue *Berlin, S. Fischer Verlag.* 1926

DEUTSCHE ANSPRACHE: Ein Appell an die Vernunft
  Lecture   *Berlin, S. Fischer Verlag.*   1930

DIE FORDERUNG DES TAGES
  Essays   *Berlin, S. Fischer Verlag.*   1930

MARIO UND DER ZAUBERER
  [Mario and the Magician]. Short novel
                                    Berlin, S. Fischer Verlag.   1930

GOETHE ALS REPRÄSENTANT DES BÜRGERLICHEN ZEITALTERS
  Lecture   *Berlin, S. Fischer Verlag.*   1932

JOSEPH UND SEINE BRÜDER
  [Joseph and His Brothers]. Novel
    I. Die Geschichten Jaakobs. 1933   *Berlin, S. Fischer*
                                          Verlag.
    II. Der junge Joseph. 1934   *Berlin, S. Fischer Verlag.*
    III. Joseph in Ägypten. 1936   *Vienna, Bermann-Fischer*
                                          Verlag.
    IV. Joseph, der Ernährer. 1943
                        Stockholm, Bermann-Fischer Verlag.

LEIDEN UND GRÖSSE DER MEISTER
  Essays   *Berlin, S. Fischer Verlag.*   1935

FREUD UND DIE ZUKUNFT
  Lecture   *Vienna, Bermann-Fischer Verlag.*   1936

EIN BRIEFWECHSEL
  [An Exchange of Letters]
                        Zurich, Dr. Oprecht & Helbling AG.   1937

81

SCHOPENHAUER
Essay   *Stockholm, Bermann-Fischer Verlag.* 1938

ACHTUNG, EUROPA!
Manifesto   *Stockholm, Bermann-Fischer Verlag.* 1938

DIE SCHÖNSTEN ERZÄHLUNGEN
Contains *Tonio Kröger, Der Tod in Venedig, Unordnung und frühes Leid, Mario und der Zauberer*
                         Stockholm, Bermann-Fischer Verlag. 1938

DAS PROBLEM DER FREIHEIT
Essay   *Stockholm, Bermann-Fischer Verlag.* 1939

LOTTE IN WEIMAR
[The Beloved Returns]. Novel
                         Stockholm, Bermann-Fischer Verlag. 1939

DIE VERTAUSCHTEN KÖPFE: Eine indische Legende
[The Transposed Heads: A Legend of India]
                         Stockholm, Bermann-Fischer Verlag. 1940

DEUTSCHE HÖRER
[Listen, Germany!] Broadcasts
                         Stockholm, Bermann-Fischer Verlag. 1942

DAS GESETZ
[The Tables of the Law]
                         Stockholm, Bermann-Fischer Verlag. 1944

DOKTOR FAUSTUS: DAS LEBEN DES DEUTSCHEN TONSETZERS
   ADRIAN LEVERKÜHN, ERZÄHLT VON EINEM FREUNDE
Novel   *Stockholm, Bermann-Fischer Verlag.* 1947

DER ERWÄHLTE
[The Holy Sinner]. Novel
Frankfurt am Main, S. Fischer Verlag. 1951

DIE BETROGENE
[The Black Swan]. Short Novel
Frankfurt am Main, S. Fischer Verlag. 1953

ALTES UND NEUES: Kleine Prosa aus fünf Jahrzehnten.
[Small prose pieces of five decades]
Frankfurt am Main, S. Fischer Verlag. 1953

BEKENNTNISSE DES HOCHSTAPLERS FELIX KRULL: DER ME-
MOIREN ERSTER TEIL
[Confessions of Felix Krull]. Novel
Frankfurt am Main, S. Fischer Verlag. 1954

NACHLESE: Prosa 1951–1955
Frankfurt am Main, S. Fischer Verlag. 1956

BRIEFE
1889–1936   1961
1937–1947   1963
1948–1955 UND NACHLESE   1965
Frankfurt am Main, S. Fischer Verlag.

American Editions in Translation

published by ALFRED A. KNOPF, *New York*

ROYAL HIGHNESS: A NOVEL OF GERMAN COURT LIFE
Translated by A. Cecil Curtis   1916

BUDDENBROOKS
   Translated H. T. Lowe-Porter   1924

DEATH IN VENICE AND OTHER STORIES
   Translated by Kenneth Burke. Contains Der Tod in
   Venedig, Tristan, *and* Tonio Kröger (*out of print*)*   1925

THE MAGIC MOUNTAIN
   Translated by H. T. Lowe-Porter. Two volumes   1927

CHILDREN AND FOOLS
   Translated by Herman George Scheffauer. Nine stories,
   including translations of Der kleine Herr Friedemann
   and Unordnung und frühes Leid (*out of print*)*   1928

THREE ESSAYS
   Translated by H. T. Lowe-Porter. Contains translations
   of Friedrich und die grosse Koalition *from* Rede und
   Antwort, *and of* Goethe und Tolstoi *and* Okkulte Er-
   lebnisse *from* Bemühungen (*out of print*)   1929

EARLY SORROW
   Translated by Herman George Scheffauer (*out of print*)*   1930

A MAN AND HIS DOG
   Translated by Herman George Scheffauer (*out of print*)*   1930

---

* Included in *Stories of Three Decades*, translated by H. T. Lowe-Porter.

DEATH IN VENICE
  *A new translation by H. T. Lowe-Porter, with an Intro-
  duction by Ludwig Lewisohn (out of print)**   1930

MARIO AND THE MAGICIAN
  *Translated by H. T. Lowe-Porter (out of print)**   1931

PAST MASTERS AND OTHER PAPERS
  Translated by H. T. Lowe-Porter (out of print)   1933

JOSEPH AND HIS BROTHERS
  I. Joseph and His Brothers (The Tales of Jacob)   1934
  II. Young Joseph   1935
  III. Joseph in Egypt   1938
  IV. Joseph the Provider   1944

  The complete work in 1 volume   1948
  Translated by H. T. Lowe-Porter

STORIES OF THREE DECADES
  *Translated by H. T. Lowe-Porter. Contains all of
  Thomas Mann's fiction prior to 1940 except the long
  novels*   1936

AN EXCHANGE OF LETTERS
  Translated by H. T. Lowe-Porter (out of print)   1937

---

* Included in *Stories of Three Decades*, translated by H. T. Lowe-Porter.

FREUD, GOETHE, WAGNER
  *Translated by H. T. Lowe-Porter and Rita Matthias-
  Reil. Three essays (out of print)*   1937

THE COMING VICTORY OF DEMOCRACY
  Translated by Agnes E. Meyer (out of print)   1938

THIS PEACE
  Translated by H. T. Lowe-Porter (out of print)   1938

THIS WAR
  Translated by Eric Sutton (out of print)   1940

THE BELOVED RETURNS
  [Lotte in Weimar]
  Translated by H. T. Lowe-Porter   1940

THE TRANSPOSED HEADS: A LEGEND OF INDIA
  Translated by H. T. Lowe-Porter   1941

ORDER OF THE DAY
  Political Essays and Speeches of Two Decades
  *Translated by H. T. Lowe-Porter, Agnes E. Meyer, and
  Eric Sutton (out of print)*   1942

LISTEN, GERMANY!
  Twenty-five Radio Messages to the German People over
  BBC *(out of print)*   1943

THE TABLES OF THE LAW
  Translated by H. T. Lowe-Porter   1945

ESSAYS OF THREE DECADES
  Translated by H. T. Lowe-Porter   1947

DOCTOR FAUSTUS: THE LIFE OF THE GERMAN COMPOSER
  ADRIAN LEVERKÜHN AS TOLD BY A FRIEND
  Translated by H. T. Lowe-Porter   1948

THE HOLY SINNER
  Translated by H. T. Lowe-Porter   1951

THE BLACK SWAN
  Translated by Williard R. Trask   1954

CONFESSIONS OF FELIX KRULL, CONFIDENCE MAN: THE
  EARLY YEARS
  Translated by Denver Lindley   1955

LAST ESSAYS
  Translated by Richard and Clara Winston and Tania
  and James Stern   1959

A SKETCH OF MY LIFE
  Translated by H. T. Lowe-Porter   1960

THE STORY OF A NOVEL: THE GENESIS OF DOCTOR
  FAUSTUS
  Translated by Richard and Clara Winston   1961

DEATH IN VENICE
  A new edition of Kenneth Burke's translation   1965

87

A Note about the Author

THOMAS MANN, born in 1875 into one of Lübeck's prominent merchant families, was only twenty-five when *Buddenbrooks* was published. His second great work of fiction, *The Magic Mountain*, was issued in 1924. Five years later he was awarded the Nobel Prize for Literature.

The chance request of an artist for an introduction to a portfolio of Joseph drawings was the genesis of his tetralogy, *Joseph and His Brothers*, the first volume of which was published in 1933. In that same year Mann left Munich—where he had made his home—and Germany, to settle for a time in Switzerland.

After several visits to the United States, he came to live in Princeton, New Jersey, where he lectured at the university. In 1940 his Goethe novel, *The Beloved Returns*, appeared.

In 1941 Mann moved to Pacific Palisades, California. It was there that he wrote *Doctor Faustus* and *The Holy Sinner*. Three years later he became a citizen of the United States. In 1952 he moved to Kilchberg, a suburb of Zurich. There he wrote *Confessions of Felix Krull, Confidence Man*, the continuation of a fragmentary story that had been published more than thirty years earlier. He died in 1955, not long after a memorable three-day celebration of his eightieth birthday.

A Note on the Type

The text of this book was set on the Linotype in Janson, *a recutting made direct from the type cast from matrices long thought to have been made by Anton Janson, a Dutchman who was a practising type-founder in Leipzig during the years 1668–1687. However, it has been conclusively demonstrated that these types are actually the work of Nicholas Kis (1650–1702), a Hungarian who learned his trade most probably from the master Dutch type-founder Dirk Voskens.*

This type is an excellent example of the influential and sturdy Dutch types that prevailed in England prior to the development by William Caslon of his own incomparable designs, which he evolved from these Dutch faces. The Dutch in their turn had been influenced by Claude Garamond in France. The general tone of the Janson, however, is darker than Garamond and has a sturdiness and substance quite different from its predecessors.

Composed, printed, and bound by Kingsport Press, Inc., Kingsport, Tenn. Paper manufactured by P. H. Glatfelter Co., Spring Grove, Pa. Typography and binding design by George Salter.

THOMAS MANN
A Sketch of My Life

Published in a very limited edition as far back as 1930, this fascinating narrative is for the first time available to all who wish to read it. Here Thomas Mann tells the story of a young solitary's rise to world fame; he gives a delightful account of a youthful celebrity's achievement of personal happiness; and he reports on the growing involvement of the middle-aged man and artist with the demands of his times.

Many of the questions that have puzzled students of Mann's work and life are taken up in these pages, with gratifying directness: his awareness of a story-teller's obligations toward society; the seeming dichotomy between the urgings of his sense of duty and the pleasure afforded him by his own "playful" occupations; the peculiar "rhythm" of his inventive capacities; and the altogether enigmatic felicity with which new subjects presented themselves to his imagination.

Some of his greatest triumphs and all his great trials lay ahead of him when he wrote this memoir. But all the *leitmotifs* of his life are present in it; and, for all the conversational informality of the writing, they are as much "in their proper places" as any of the significant scenes in his great novels.